My Little
Family Prayer Book

by Maïte Roche

CTS Children's Books

In the name of the Father,
and of the Son, and of the Holy Spirit.

Lord, bless my family:
my Daddy and my Mummy,
my Grandfathers and my Grandmothers.
Lord, bless all the children,
from the littlest to the biggest:
brothers and sisters,
cousins and friends.
Bless every family in the world.
Keep our hearts full of joy
like on a wedding day.

Amen.

In the name of the Father,
and of the Son, and of the Holy Spirit.

Alleluia!
Give glory to God, our Father,
for the life he gives us.
For my Baptism, alleluia!
For my Godmother and Godfather, alleluia!
For the great family of God's children, alleluia!
Glory to God!

Amen.

In the name of the Father,
and of the Son, and of the Holy Spirit.

Jesus, Mary and Joseph,
God's holy Family,
pray for us.
Help us to serve
one another,
and to do the
little everyday things
with love.

Amen.

In the name of the Father,
and of the Son, and of the Holy Spirit.

I'm sorry, Jesus,
for quarrelling
and being cross and unkind.
Teach us to make friends again
and love each other.
Give us a clean, new heart
to bring peace and joy, just like you.

Amen.

In the name of the Father,
and of the Son, and of the Holy Spirit.

Thank you, Lord,
for the cake my Mummy made.
Thank you for Daddy's smile.
Thank you for my lovely home.
Thank you for our birthday meal.
Thank you for the joy of being together.
Thank you, Lord, for my family!

Amen.

In the name of the Father,
and of the Son, and of the Holy Spirit.

Lord,
make us live and grow
in your Spirit of love.
Welcome into your dwelling-place
in the happiness of your Kingdom
all those who have died and left this life.
You love us forever and ever,
so I entrust to your care my family,
and the people I have in my heart.

Amen.

In the name of the Father,
and of the Son, and of the Holy Spirit.

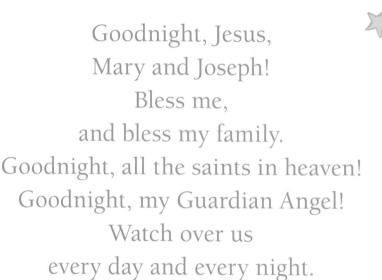

Goodnight, Jesus,
Mary and Joseph!
Bless me,
and bless my family.
Goodnight, all the saints in heaven!
Goodnight, my Guardian Angel!
Watch over us
every day and every night.

Amen.

15

CTS Children's Books

The Beautiful Story of Jesus, by Maïte Roche (CTS Code CH 13)

The Beautiful Story of Mary, by Maïte Roche (CTS Code CH 37)

The Beautiful Story of the Bible, by Maïte Roche (CTS Code CH 27)

The Bible for little children, by Maïte Roche (CTS Code CH 2)

First prayers for little children, by Maïte Roche (CTS Code CH 5)

The Gospel for little children, by Maïte Roche (CTS Code CH 1)

The most beautiful Christmas Story, by Maïte Roche (CTS Code CH 8)

My Little Christmas Prayer Book, by Maïte Roche (CTS Code CH 31)

My Little Missal, by Maïte Roche (CTS Code CH 20)

Text and illustrations by Maïte Roche
Translated by Helena Scott

My Little Family Prayer Book: Published 2011 by The Incorporated Catholic Truth Society, 40-46 Harleyford Road, London SE11 5AY. Tel: 020 7640 0042; Fax: 020 7640 0046; www.cts-online.org.uk. Copyright © 2011 The Incorporated Catholic Truth Society in this English-language edition.

ISBN: 978 1 86082 763 1   CTS Code CH 38

Original title **Premières prières pour ma famille:** ISBN 978-2-7289-1316-9 © Fleurus-Mame, 2010.